Living

Positive steps to manage stress

and

achieve peace of mind

Martin Stepek

ISBN:978-0-9556507-9-6

Published by
Fleming Publications
Fleming House
Glasgow

Contents

Introduction

In July of 2011 I started delivering a weekly mindfulness class in my home town, Hamilton in Scotland. I had been teaching mindfulness for seven years up to that point and I wanted to create something that would help local people try mindfulness at their convenience. I wanted it to be free and drop-in: the former so that no one would be put off coming because of financial constraints, the latter so that people might still be able to attend some of the time despite rotas for night shift work, duties such as caring for children or parents, or other important personal commitments.

With the encouragement and support of people in NHS Lanarkshire, South Lanarkshire Council and the University of the West of Scotland I was able to get the classes started. The University kindly provided me with a lecture theatre in its Hamilton campus, and all three organisations promoted the weekly sessions to their employees online. This gave the initiative a crucial early boost.

The writings in this book were originally created as articles for the weekly newsletters I sent to those who expressed an interest, many of whom come to the Hamilton class. The purpose of the newsletter was to remind people that the class was running each week, was there for their benefit, and to help readers get a sense of how to "do" mindfulness in real life away from lecture theatres and silent rooms. For the most part in the articles, I didn't attempt to describe the classic meditative process expounded by so many mindfulness books in recent years. Instead I focussed on how to be mindful in everyday situations. How do you deal with trying to be mindful while watching television? What are the feelings we experience when supporting a sporting hero? Are these feelings healthy or unhealthy? Can we do anything about the unhelpful feelings when we notice their destructive nature?

Many of the people who attend my classes suggested that I compile the articles and make a book out of them, so this publication is in direct response to such requests. I have read maybe over a hundred books on mindfulness or books which contain chapters on the subject. Most are very clear but tend to be somewhat dry. This is inevitable as mindfulness is something you do, not something to learn. Or rather you learn insights through doing it. So trying to understand mindfulness through reading books, no matter how clearly written, is a bit like trying to experience Paris through memorising a map of the city. The only way to experience a city is to go there. Similarly the only way to experience mindfulness is to do it.

There are two ways of doing mindfulness. One is the classic mindfulness "meditation". I put quotation marks around "meditation" as I don't like the word. Some people hear "meditation" and want to run a mile from it. Others are drawn towards it thinking it will bring them everlasting peace or some kind of spiritual transformation.

There are a thousand different interpretations of what is meant by meditation so I avoid using the word as much as I can. A word with so many different meanings and capable of invoking polarised responses is not a very useful word. However its use is very common in the field of mindfulness, hence my use of it here, if only to urge you to ignore it. The original term bhavana was so much closer to the mark. It means development. It's as simple as that, citta-bhavana – the development of the mind or consciousness. Mindfulness is about mental development, from a core of two deeply ethical states, compassion for others and a firm commitment to try to avoid causing harm.

This book doesn't explain how to do the classic mindfulness practice of sitting quietly. If you are coming to mindfulness for the first time I suggest you go onto You Tube and type "mindfulness" in the Search space. You'll find dozens of fabulous videos explaining what it is, how to do it, and all sorts of actual practices to try for yourself.

Instead this book seeks to give practitioners of mindfulness an insight into one person's moment by moment, day by day responses to life as they have arisen through the best part of a year and how that individual (me) tried to handle common experiences mindfully, acknowledging slips and falls and imperfections—sometimes reflecting with hindsight how situations might have been better resolved, but always without being drawn into unhelpful emotions such as regret or frustration. There is a significant difference between sitting quietly observing the breath and the mind for a sustained length of time and being mindful in everyday moments. Sitting in a quiet room practising mindfulness is akin to pre-season training for a sport. It enables a person to get familiar with the way the mind operates; how it can be easily distracted by sounds, thoughts, ingrained habits or daydreams and how it can, despite this, attain a profound and nurturing sense of peace and stillness.

Being mindful in everyday life is like playing the sport itself rather than training. Life is only possible in the present moment; the only time we can experience what it is to be alive. Yet so often we miss it almost completely because our mind is functioning on automatic pilot, directed without our consent by decades-old habits, or tendencies to produce inappropriate knee-jerk responses. Through these conditioned mental processes we only semi-live in the moment. Often we don't live at all but are like zombies —going through the motions, having experiences but not noticing them. Being mindful is the skill of allowing the mind to be empty, fresh and alive to the fullness of the moment, to see it as if you had never seen it before, even if the moment is simply looking out of the window at your own driveway.

This is the one sport or game we all play. It's called life and we only get a single crack at it. Moreover life is composed of billions of these individual moments of time and place. They are so ephemeral, so fleeting that even if we are extremely mindful we'll still miss millions of them. That's not a problem. The prize is to be fully aware and alive for as many of them as our trained mind can capture. That is life. With a fresh clear still mind we can see the unlimited potential in a single moment, the opportunity to soak in as much as life has to offer in that moment, and equally importantly for our true fulfilment, to give lovingly and generously to the world just as it is in that moment. To do this is to live fully, to be perfect if only for that fleeting moment.

Numerous scientific studies attest to the powerful benefits mindfulness practice can bring to us. From prevention of recurrences of depression and suicidal thoughts, to clearer decision-making and wider oversight by leaders, mindfulness can be seen as a remarkable ethical tool for nurturing our finest human qualities and neutralising our destructive or unhealthy tendencies, feelings and mental habits. However, it's an ongoing game of cat and mouse between our wiser mind and the automatic habit-driven mind. It's a game that cannot be won by force, will-power or suppression of thoughts but only by subtle, gentle patient attention and calmness. Moreover it is really the only game that matters, the only game in town. This short book can be considered a commentary on my own game of life, recorded in writing almost in real-time, plus a series of helpful tips from one individual who plays the game to win the beautiful prize, full awakening to the wonders of being alive. At the end of this game we all die. No more moments. No going back and replaying time. It's over. So I hope this little book, designed to be portable for your practical use day to day will help you experience more of this marvellous adventure of life and help keep you from the harmful or negative delusions all of our minds create from time to time.

PART 1

WORK AND LIFE
Reflections on being happy in real life

Dealing with work overload

Many people feel very stressed about the amount of tasks they have to get done by a particular time, whether the work relates to their job or their home and family life. The stress, worry and mental unrest are very real and unhealthy but the cause, too much to get done, is not.

As always it's a delusion, a "thing" created by our minds in response to the situation. Let's look at the reality from a purely mindfulness perspective.

Mindfulness reminds us that there is only right now, this moment. Everything else is imagined by our minds. The past is gone; what we think of as memories are subjectively edited highlights or lowlights. The future has not yet occurred. What we often do is try to plan the future, worry about it or imagine good things that might come our way but all we ever have to play with, to actually experience or to use to get something done, is the moment.

Another thing mindfulness reminds us of, is the fact that the mind can only do one thing at a time. What we call multi-tasking is actually flitting about at high speed from one thing to another; not usually the best way to get anything done at high quality, but definitely a good way to feel frazzled, tired, and snappy by the end of the day.

So let's take these two mindful insights together. There is only the present moment, and we can only do one thing at a time. What does this tell us about overwork and stress?

It shows there is, in reality, no such thing as overwork. You can only work in the present moment and you can only do one thing then. Hence no overwork, even if you feel it's there. The only possible plan is to use the moment to assess what is the most important or urgent thing to do, then in the next moment start to do it.

Once one task is done, in the next moment you still only have one task you can do, so do the next most urgent or important and so on with each task.

If you truly see things in this way, and it is the only truthful way of seeing life, then there cannot be such a thing as overwork. There is only work, and the moment in which to do work. Of course that leaves two issues. Firstly, dealing with the stress—simply observe it with mindfulness, see it, name it, and then let it dissolve in its own time. Breathing practice helps a lot here. Secondly, maybe you have to deal with a manager about not getting something done on time—but that's another subject for another time!

Leading moments

I'm sometimes asked to do talks on leadership. Having practised mindfulness for many years, I see this subject differently from what I read in books about leadership or theories on the subject.

In my view there is no such thing as a leader. Leadership is simply making decisions including, crucially, how and what we communicate to others.

Every one of us makes decisions at each moment we are awake, whether that decision is to keep watching the television or whether, as President, we should arm Syrian rebels, it's still a decision. Each moment asks of us a response. When we are with others—face to face or virtually through email, the telephone, or social media, we have to listen, read, and respond in words or gestures.

When we look at things deeply, with mindfulness, we see that there is only ever the present moment, and our only task ever is to respond to the reality of that present moment, hence the title of this piece—Leading Moments.

No one leads people. All we can do is respond to the moment. How we respond depends on our quality of mind at that particular moment. Is it tired, anxious, depressed, angry, bitter? If it is any of these our response, our decision, our communication, our "leadership" is likely to be tainted by these destructive or unhelpful states of mind. If on the other hand the mind is clear, calm, alert, considerate, compassionate, thinking of the good of all then our response to the moment, that moment of leadership, is highly likely to be constructive, helpful, and long-term in its nature.

Mindfulness trains us first of all to simply see—to see our state of mind at the moment. It then trains us to calmly but quickly assess whether that state of mind is likely to result in a healthy response. If not we simply observe the mind and, as all thoughts or emotions eventually do, the existing thought fades away. This leaves us with a clearer and calmer mind from which to make a more considered response.

What we call leadership is usually just related to a position of power—appointed or elected. We are impressed by stirring words from charismatic people but in reality these leaders have moment by moment choices to make just as we do.

So please lead your life. Lead this moment and the next. Practice mindfulness to let go of destructive or unhelpful habits of thought and cultivate your mind so that it is increasingly clear, calm and kind-hearted when decisions have to be made and when words have to be spoken or written.

Don't take time out. Take time in.

Every so often we feel we need a break during the day. We call it a coffee break—time out. We do this whether we're at home or at work. Usually this becomes a habit, a kind of ritual in our lives. Same time each day, same actions—pour a coffee, a cup of tea, maybe take a biscuit or cake—if at home the TV gets switched on or we catch up with Facebook. It's part of the rhythm of the day.

I suggest you try a new version of this. Not time out, time in—time that, when you need a break, you don't immediately and instinctively reach for external pick-me-ups like coffee, tea or the mobile phone. Instead just close your eyes, sit in a comfortable upright and balanced way, do a quick one minute scan through all your main body parts to relax them, and focus purely and gently on your breath, almost as if you are observing it in slow motion, catching each single moment of the in-breath, then each moment of the out-breath.

Feel your body regain its energy. Feel your mind slow down, become calm, refreshed, re-energised. In this way, without words or thinking, you remind yourself that you matter, that your physical and mental wellbeing is a priority in your life. You also remind yourself that the moment is precious, that it is always, your whole life, the only time you can be fully alive to all that life presents at that time. Try not to miss your life.

Then, if you have time, I'd recommend nipping outside for two minutes of gentle walking, breathing in the freshness of the air outside—and if there's still time, get into the habit of having a green tea. The scientists say it is very good for you—or drink some cool water from the tap. That's a mindful break. Enjoy your day.

Not really listening

Of my many weaknesses and imperfections poor listening at home must be up there with the worst. I suspect I'm not alone in this. It's not that I'm a poor listener in my work or with my friends. At work especially, people have told me how much they appreciate the degree to which I listen and empathise.

It's something about home. More specifically, it's something about the living room. Not just my living room, most living rooms.

Living rooms, a long time ago, probably were living rooms. Places where people got together for a while. Now it's where the forty inch flat screen TV dominates the other forms of technology—laptop, Wii, DVD collection and myriad games consoles. It's not really a living room any longer, more an entertainments venue. Not ideal for conversation, certainly not for listening, but where else can we listen to each other?

What is a relationship about? It's about empathy, understanding, giving. To give you have to empathise, and to empathise you have to understand, but to understand you have to listen, listen deeply.

That's really hard when the TV is on. Your partner or your kids or parents' conversation has to be incredibly interesting to win your attention when it is competing against Lionel Messi, Brad Pitt, Rihanna, or Jo Brand

—but it's not just TV, there's also our own inner entertainment channel. I'm an ideas person. I think a lot and I enjoy thinking about things. So when my wife tells me about her day she has to compete with thirty things that are going on in my head. Of course I find it difficult to drag myself away from my own thoughts, but... half-listening or non-listening is disrespectful, even insulting, especially when this might be the only time we have together all day.

For all my faults and weaknesses, my mindfulness does sometimes work in this situation. I notice that my mind has been distracted, so I bring my attention back to the conversation just as we bring it back to the breath when we do mindfulness in a class. It's the same process, just a different situation.

It's hard work but I'm getting better at paying more attention to my wife and kids when they talk to me, and it brings you closer. Just that little effort of being fully aware for a few seconds more each time changes the relationship, nurturing it little by little, so that as the years go by you become closer. That's what relationships are supposed to do.

Knowing what to do and not do

We often see it in the papers—an example happened just the other day. Saturated fat, according to one research scientist, is not actually bad for you. We all think, not again, they keep changing their advice on good health practices.

Such apparent changes in understanding can make us either uncertain as to what to do in daily life, or worse, makes us so cynical that we just ignore any advice because we don't trust it any longer. What are we to do?

A cynic dismisses everything, and in doing so, loses out on some vital lessons in life. A sceptic on the other hand wants to see objective evidence before they decide. I'm on the sceptic's side, I want to know, "where's the proof?". Mindfulness asks us to be sceptical, that is, to keep an open mind, but check the evidence, always check the evidence.

This is especially true when what we're looking at is our own thoughts, opinions or feelings. Think about the word, mindful, it's about being aware, taking in the fullness of what's happening. That's evidence-gathering, that's trying to see as fully as we can.

The great attraction of mindfulness for me was that the scientific evidence backed what I felt mindfulness was actually doing for those who practised it. There are now over 2500 academic research papers on the benefits of mindfulness. Here are summaries of the main findings from mostly very recent papers:

☐ effective treatment for reducing anxiety and mood symptoms (2013, Neuroimage)
☐ decreases loneliness in older adults (2012, Brain, Behaviour and Immunity)
☐ reduces cravings in smokers (2013, Social, Cognitive and Affective Neuroscience)
☐ curtails distress and enhances mental health physical health, and behaviour regulation (2007, Psychological Inquiry)

Just four of the thousands of papers showing the wide range and depth of benefits from practising mindfulness. Over 400 papers have been published each year recently, so the evidence is still growing and more and more benefits are being discovered.

There are three ways of looking at the benefits of mindfulness—healing, prevention, and nurturing. The "deficit" view, concerned with what goes wrong with people, uses mindfulness to get them out of poor states of mind such as depression. The preventative approach helps people remain free from stress, depression, anxiety, anger etc. However, little is said about the third area—helping people increase their sense of joy, happiness, love of life, and care for each other, year in year out for the rest of their lives. I think there's massive potential for you in working in this direction. Now that's not cynical!

Thoughts and words, the connection

Our thoughts create for us our view of the world—how we see it. If we're in a grumpy mood we don't see a beautiful joyous place but rather a dour unpleasant one, or we don't see anything at all because our mood so blinkers what we can see.

If we're feeling happy, excited, or just plain content the world becomes for us somewhere special and we feel good about it.

Neither view is real. The world just is. It has no adjective like "lovely" or "terrible" fixed to it. We, or rather, our minds add the mood. The point therefore is not to try to find the True View of our world, but much more practically, to nurture our mind so that it perceives a view that is healthy, uplifting, energising for our own lives—and for the people around us—family, friends, work colleagues, neighbours. Who wants a grumpy person for company?

When it comes to words, those crucial tools of communication, who wants to hear what a grumpy, cynical, or negative person has to say?

What we say comes from what we think or how we feel. Whether it's an email, text message, work report or just a casual conversation, the words that come out, their tone, their message, is the direct result of our own mind in that moment. Thus it follows, if you want to be a good communicator, don't focus primarily on the words to use, or on honing certain skills to do with mastering body language techniques or using the right tone. All these forms of communication emerge naturally from your frame of mind. Don't fake communication, change things where it really matters, in your own mind.

Everyone should try to communicate well, because words are so important. Poor communication is the most common thing people complain about in the workplace, and is cited as a major cause of many relationship breakdowns.

To communicate well, focus on mindfulness, staying on top of what emerges from your mind, letting go of the negative, nurturing what helps you flourish. Better communication will flow naturally from that.

This does not mean ignoring the real woes of this world, nor pretending they don't exist but it does mean taking an energised optimistic approach to such problems. Why? Because, firstly, such a frame of mind makes you more productive and capable, so if you determine to be active in any social justice cause then you have the best frame of mind to be effective in it and secondly, a negative frame of mind damages you both mentally and physically in the long-term, so it is a form of self-harming.

So—communicate better by nurturing your mind.

Television and Mindfulness

Television is amazing. In my lifetime it has given me huge amounts of humour, laughter, drama, excitement, beauty, education, and much more, but there's a downside. Television often brings out the opposite of mindfulness in each of us. It can put us into a deep autopilot from which it is difficult to exit, so we watch programme after programme.

I think there are two features of TV which cause this effect. The first is the nature of most programmes. They typically feature good-looking people and exciting content, whether that's thriller, drama, love, murder, or whatever. Unless you're James Bond that means that what you're doing in real life at that moment pales into insignificance compared to what's going on in the TV programme, so you get drawn in to it.

The other aspect of TV that causes us to go into autopilot is that it is a one-way process. We are the passive recipients of entertainment. The programmes need nothing from us other than that we watch and listen. We don't discuss with the TV, we don't explore issues, exchange views, and we can't reach out and hug that person who has just learned bad news in the soap opera. In a strange way it enthrals us while switching parts of our minds off completely.

Mindfulness asks us to be clearly and calmly aware of what's going on in the present moment, but it is very difficult to be mindful of what's going on in real life when an amazing drama is simultaneously capturing your attention in the living room on TV.

We are understandably drawn to the screen and away from anyone we are with or anything else we're doing. Let's face it however interesting our closest friend or partner might be, they are not Johnny Depp sword-fencing, or Homer Simpson about to screw up for the millionth time. So family and friends lose out through our inattention to them. That's not great but surely it's ok once in a while? Except it's not once in a while.

The average person watches four hours of TV every day. That's between a quarter and a fifth of our waking day. For an average person living seventy to eighty years of age that's fourteen to twenty years of their life just watching TV. Fourteen to twenty years potentially ignoring your loved ones. Fourteen to twenty whole years when you could have been doing something, or just being aware of the fullness of life in a truly mindful way.

Television is great. I don't suggest giving it up, but it is not the same as living. Try mindfully watching a programme with others so it's shared time. Switch off a regular show and just chat, go for a walk, or practise mindfulness. Try it—see what happens.

Here and now

Mindfulness is two things: it is the skill of remembering to pay attention to the present moment without judgement or inner commentary and it is also the insights we gain from doing these paying attention practices. Ultimately mindfulness becomes much more than the practices. Through the insights we gain, mindfulness changes how we see ourselves, our world, and our relationship to the world. It becomes a way of being, a different, less hurried, more appreciative, and more compassionate way of being.

We can only be mindful in the present moment and the present moment has two parts. One is now, in other words a moment of time and the other is here, the physical place where we happen to be.

Much of the focus of mindfulness is on the now part. This is because we spend much of our waking time thinking about the future, planning for it, reminding ourselves about the things we have to do next, worrying about being late for something, worrying that it won't go well, anxious that things will always go wrong. Thus we dwell on the future and miss the present, the here and the now, the place we are and the only moment we can experience life. Or we dwell on the past, whether the very recent past, such as when we brood on an incident or an argument or something someone said to us earlier in the

25

day, or going way back years or decades, still being bitter or resentful about something someone did in the distant past. We carry the pain and burden and energy-sapping qualities of those moods and emotions with us in those moments—and thus the moments are lost to us. We don't experience here, and we let now fritter away.

Spend a few moments now focussing on 'here'—wherever you are right now. Notice where you are and what it is—a building, an office, a room in a house? What colour are the walls? Are there any things in the room? What? What do you have available here that most of humanity doesn't have, or that most of the people in history never had the chance to enjoy or use or experience—central heating for example? Just notice, be aware of where you are.

If you have a window look out of it. What's around you? Ask the same questions about what's outside as you did for what's in your room. Just notice things and how you respond to what you see or hear or smell.

The reality is, for all its many problems and issues, we live in a time of incredible luxury and technology which we take for granted and which keeps us absorbed yet all around us are an almost infinite variety of natural features, from grass, trees, clouds and wind, to temperatures whether cold or mild or warm. Try to take time as often as you can to be right here and fully present in the now.

Stuck and unstuck

The human mind likes order. It likes stability and routine. That's why it creates habits. This allows us to learn things quickly then no longer need to think about them. Learning to drive is the great example. From the first lessons when we find it so hard to co-ordinate using the pedals, steering wheel, gear stick and handbrake, we eventually find ourselves driving without a second thought. The mind has learned the method and allows us to drive safely without having to think consciously at all.

Many of our habits and skills are learned and developed in the same way. We had to learn how to walk, swim, play sport, games, knit, and a thousand other activities all to our benefit.

However it's not only physical activities that become routine. Our personality traits are made routine in much the same way. Some of these habits are healthy for us and those around us—kindness, consideration, respect, harmless humour, tolerance. These are all trained habits, learned just as we learned to walk, but some of our habits or traits are destructive or unhelpful. Aggression, quick-temperedness, tendency to worry or be anxious, over-planning, becoming depressed, a manic mind that never lets us rest. These, too, are learned behaviours.

Similarly we can become institutionalised, in our workplace or in our local or national culture. Some of this may be harmless such as supporting the same football team for life, even though the manager, players and football strips all change periodically. But it may not be harmless—perhaps hating the other team and their supporters is part of the same mental habit. We can become stuck or encrusted by these habits. Working in the same career or at the same workplace for a long time can make us stuck mentally in a particular way of working, or doing, or even how we identify ourselves. Unless we act.

Just as our muscles need stretched or they tighten up and we become less flexible and supple, the same is true for our minds. The mind needs to be regularly decluttered, loosened up, disentangled, unstuck. A mind that is fluid and flexible sees the beauty of life, sees the harm and nonsense that the mind naturally produces, and allows such thoughts and emotions to dissipate harmlessly.

This is essentially what mindfulness is ultimately about—liberating the mind from unhealthy mental states and breaking up those fossilised, hardened views. A clear, calm, happy mind can deal with anything that life throws at it without becoming stuck in negativity, narrow opinions or unpleasant personality traits. So, do the practice... right now.

There is no such thing as normal

Last week I finally was able to focus once again on my work, fully five weeks after the death of my father, then my mother. It was a pleasure, almost a relief to get back to something comparatively stable and familiar. An attempt to get back to normal, but when I reflected on it with some mindfulness it struck me that there is no such thing as "normal." In fact it can sometimes be unhelpful to think in that term. Every moment is rich with potential. Every moment is unique. When we think of things as "normal" there's a real chance we'll slip straight into automatic pilot. By doing so we may drop our mindfulness of what is possible in this moment and revert to our habitual, unthinking way of dealing with a familiar situation.

Right now the sun is pouring through my office window. I can think of it as annoying as its brightness hits my eyes. That's my habitual way of thinking of this situation. But it is also warm, somehow uplifting, maybe because there's an inch and a half of snow outside so the twin effect of snow and ice is bright, clear and sharp. None of these views, sunlight as annoying or sunlight as uplifting is accurate in any objective way. Sunlight just is—but how much better is it for my frame of mind to accept seeing it in a positive light rather than a negative one? In this way, a small way, but a transformative one nonetheless, I have abandoned "normal" for a better, healthier and happier way of seeing this moment in the midst of grief.

Dealing with over-planning

One of the most common complaints we hear is that we're all just too busy; that we don't have time for the important things in life.

Much of this arises around the highly-planned nature of our lives, especially for those who are in work. It's not bad in itself; I have always found it helpful to have routines and a structure to the day but too much structure can kill any sense of spontaneity and freshness in your life.

A related tendency is trying to squeeze too much into a day, something I find myself doing frequently. As ever there's a healthy balance, and each of us has to work this out for ourselves. At different stages in our lives we have more or less time on our hands. The ages when we have children at home or elderly parents to care for, or both at the same time, can be the years when we feel we just don't have the opportunity to relax at all.

One of the problems with a planned day or week is that we constantly check the plan, look at our schedule to ensure that we're on track, that we haven't forgotten something, that we're going to get something done to the right standard and on time. It's at times like this we can see that our schedule is running our life rather than us managing our schedule. Mindfulness can help enormously in deceptively simple, seemingly tiny ways. All it takes to enable us to get out of this over-planning, anxiously checking mode is to take a walk outside for five minutes, even in the centre of a major city.

There's something refreshing about the combination of a sense of wider, bigger space, an array of direct and subtle noises from all directions and at all levels from loud to very quiet, and the freshness of the natural temperature of the air on the face and hands. Just being outside our comfortable homes or offices for a few minutes can recharge our batteries, rest our anxieties, free us from the planning for a few moments.

Even more so if we consciously practise pure gentle awareness of sound, our skin's response to the air, sights such as the clouds in the sky or the tops of buildings. If we breathe softly in and out and just be with the flow of the breath outside in the open air we can get rid of almost all the tension of the over-planned mind.

Try to use this as an antidote to that sense of over-busyness. It's short, it's simple and it works.

PART 2

EMOTIONS, FEELINGS, MOODS

Andy Murray,
mindfulness and skilful emotions

I watched the Wimbledon's Men's Finals on Sunday and loved it. Well, loved it doesn't describe the range of emotions and feelings I went through, particularly in the last game.

For those who didn't watch, or who aren't interested in sport, bear with me. This piece is about being able to choose our emotional responses to moments, not about the game itself.

The last game was very unusual. Andy Murray won the first three points to lead 40-0. This meant he needed just one more point to win the match and become the first British person for almost 80 years to win the Men's Singles title at Wimbledon. But Andy then lost each of the next three points, any one of which would have given him the title. Worse was to follow. He then allowed his opponent to get to the position of being within one point of winning the game, not once but three times. A win for the opponent at this stage would have turned the whole impetus of the game away from Andy.

At each of these points Andy won the point, saving the game, then finally, at the fourth attempt he won the point to seal the match and win the title.

In the last moments I was tense, frustrated, disappointed, then finally elated. I was in tears of joy for Andy Murray. Such a range of emotions in so few minutes.

Was this right for someone purporting to be mindful? Was this being mindful at all? Absolutely! Mindfulness is not about having no emotions, nor about being serene, calm, quiet at every moment. It is about fully experiencing life, with one major exception. We should seek to be so aware of our thoughts and emotions that we do not allow them to harm or hurt ourselves or others.

The tennis match yesterday was an opportunity to feel heightened emotions in a space where these feelings could be expressed, experienced and yes, enjoyed without any harmful effects.

No TV screens were smashed. No nasty comments were made about the umpire or opponent. It was a memorable moment in Scottish and British sporting history shared with my family. I thought of my recently deceased mother, thinking how she would have loved Andy's victory.

A young man, who was in his class in Dunblane when fellow pupils were shot dead at that terrible incident, had won the most famous title in tennis. His home town cheered and he brought them joy. What a wonderful gift Andy Murray gave his town.

Deep empathy

One of the great benefits of mindfulness is that it helps you achieve what Robert Burns wrote, "To see oursels as ithers see us". This as it turns out is often not very pleasant viewing. Normally our brain filters out most of our worst traits when we reflect on our own qualities, and makes spurious excuses to defend the few negative qualities that we actually do perceive. Various experiments and studies show that we have a "deceptive brain" that often seeks to present ourselves in our best light.

This may be good for morale but does not give much insight into which aspects of our thinking, feeling and behaviour we would benefit from changing. Fortunately mindfulness is a way of learning how to by-pass the deceptive brain and see, at least in part, the raw reality of what we are actually like. Thus we might see how instinctively prejudiced we are towards the opposite sex, our own sex, people from different ethnic or racial backgrounds or religions. Or we might have a skewed view of a family member, a colleague at work, or even a complete stranger we walk past in the street, simply because of the clothes or shoes they're wearing. We see when we are sarcastic, curt, rude, not listening, aggressive, dismissive in our conversations with others and we become aware when we get grumpy, tired and impatient.

And that's me after fifteen years of practising mindfulness! But the point of gathering this raw self-awareness is not to feel bad about ourselves but rather to learn what needs to be done to improve our lives. It is counter-productive to feel down or overwhelmed at the scale of our faults. Instead we can learn great insights into not just ourselves but everyone around us. As Peter Green, founder of the original Fleetwood Mac wrote in the song *Oh Well* "don't ask me what I think of you, I might not give the answer that you want me to."

In other words, within certain parameters we're all much the same, imperfect people, with flaws and unpleasant character traits. With mindfulness, over time we really do start to understand others, and not with a judgmental view but rather from a position of empathy, a sense of "I know how you feel; my mind's just as bad." It is remarkable how useful this can be in forgiving others' actions or words, and in getting along with people who in previous times we'd have run a mile from. We become more accepting of others' faults because we recognise in these our own flaws.

Empathy is the golden ingredient that prevents rows and conflicts, and is a true healer. Mindfulness nurtures empathy as well as our own inner clarity and calmness.

When something rankles

It's one of those great words—rankles. Somehow it sounds like how the mind feels when
it is in that unpleasant state.

Something rankled with me over the
weekend and I had to try to deal with it mindfully. It wasn't easy. It concerned details of a
fairly major project which involved three different parties, of which I was one. Everything
seemed to be agreed and the work finished.
Just a few tidying up things to do and it
would be job complete.

Then seemingly out of the blue one of
the two other people involved seemed to
want more than what had been discussed and
agreed. He wasn't happy with some of what
was actually done , and he wanted to add
additional work which we had not explored at
all and which seemed to me and the other
party unnecessary. Moreover he felt that we
had not shown sufficient respect or appreciation of his part in the finished work.

This rankled. It's good to see "rankled"
in one's own head. It's the first time in years
I've experienced it, and it's horrible. It
gobbles you up. It keeps cropping up in your
head and niggles away at you. All the judgemental, negative, self-pitying and aggressive
emotions come to add to the rankling. It's like
an invitation to a party for all your worst
emotions. So all through Sunday and even
Monday morning I tried not to get enveloped

by this grubby stew of negative frames of mind. I watched them, tried to gently separate out say anger from feelings of self-pity and so on. And I practised my use of breathing - breathing in "remember life's really special, don't let this stuff interfere"— breathing out, "All's good, enjoy being calm and contented".

It worked but it was hard work. As my mind finally let the whole thing drop—and it took probably about 20 mini-mindfulness techniques to loosen its grip on my mind—I could see the whole thing objectively, clearly, and compassionately from the third person's point of view.

I phoned my other collaborator and discussed the situation clearly and calmly with her. She was rankled too. We agreed a positive way forward and contacted the third party with a solution that resulted in a win-win for everyone.

The beauty of mindfulness is that it's like a tool you always have in your pocket. Our minds are programmed to sometimes give us unhealthy, harmful moods, feelings, and thoughts. That's when mindfulness pays off—not judging, just observing, paying attention to the reality of the situation, seeing it for what it really is, then applying ways to let go of what is unhelpful.

What's the weather like?

As we all know Scotland has one of the most unpredictable weather patterns in the world. It's certainly not the worst; part of Chile rarely sees rain all year round. Many places have hurricanes, typhoons, monsoons—we are spared these extremes, but the people who live in places where the weather can be truly overwhelming have at least the advantage of knowing the seasons when the worst may happen. Here in Scotland we've had snow in June and sparkling pure sunny days in January, albeit not exactly warm! And of course we're still enjoying probably the best summer any of us can remember.

However, if the weather outside is unpredictable it is nothing compared to our inner barometer. At least we see the clouds approaching. When it comes to thoughts, emotions, feelings, opinions they are lightning fast at arising. We can go from cheery to despondent in less than a second.

We have all been moved by the awful events in Syria over the past week. A common reaction is despair at human barbarity, another is anger at the perpetrators and a third is frustration at the seeming inability of governments to stop the violence. Talk about bad weather.

Or it may be something tiny in comparison to the now global problem of the war in Syria. At the weekend our youngest cat

Mia had a full-blown seizure. She ran around the living room as if possessed, then stopped and froze on her back, finally starting the classic shaking and shuddering of a fit. My wife and I were horrified and tried to help. We eventually phoned the emergency vets in Glasgow and took Mia there where she was treated and kept in overnight. By the time we got there she was fine and she has been 100% well since.

The vet explained that although the convulsions and manic actions seemed painful and terrifying, Mia, in fact, was not conscious of any of this. Her mind was effectively closed down through the whole incident, and apart from accidents such as hitting herself off a wall during the process, she was unlikely to be harmed. It was us, Christine and I, who experienced all the suffering, the panic, the consequent worry, then the relief.

So whether it is a global crisis or a domestic incident our minds are liable to be thrown into all sorts of turmoil in an instant. It's like the Scottish weather in a time-lapse film, ever-changing, from one thing to another, rarely stable for any length of time.

Mindfulness helps us in these ways:

1. It allows us to become aware of the chaotic shifts in our minds
2. Pure observation and reflection tells us that these changes are automatic, not chosen by us

3. Continued practice of mindfulness lets us see how many of these states of mind are unhelpful or just a distraction from the real choices to be made at any given time
4. With practice and familiarity we can sometimes see new states of mind arise in real time, observe them quietly, and on assessing them to be harmful or in the way, let them pass and fade away, without our getting caught up in them.
5. Equally importantly we learn to see states of mind which are nurturing, fun, and uplifting and choose to not only be absorbed by them but to make the most of them, to soak it all in and give it all out in the moment.

In these ways we can shape the weather patterns in our minds. Try it right now. Just observe your breath and see your state of mind. Think of the frame of mind you're in right now—enhance it if it's good, let it pass if it isn't. Perhaps think of the words "I feel alive" as you breathe in, and "I'm calm and contented" as you breathe out. See if it shifts anything, if it changes your frame of mind.

The weather outside is just fine. It's the weather inside your mind that determines whether your life, these precious moments right now, your experience, where you are right now, is full and rich, or gloomy and dark. Be mindful and shape your quality of mind.

Perfectly clear thinking

It was a lovely weekend. Saturday was warm and pleasant. My wife Christine and I spent time tidying the garden and on Saturday night went to see a friend's band play in a pub.

Sunday was all set to be similarly warm and enjoyable, and it started much the same way. Down the valley, time out for a coffee then back home with a little more gardening work to be done.

Then Christine's mobile rang. I was nearer so I picked it up, went outside to give it to her but noticed that it was our daughter Katie who was calling, so I answered it. It was just after noon.

She is a student at Stirling University, and stays at a flat there. She's eighteen and just started her second year. She earns her keep by working part- time at a bar-restaurant at weekends.

"I thought you needed to know I'm going to A&E." A full two litre bottle of Morgan Spice had fallen off its bracket and hit Katie on the top of her head knocking her to the floor of the pub. The bottle didn't break nor did Katie's skin or skull but she was in shock, dazed and was developing a headache.

Within half an hour we were at Forth Valley Royal Hospital and met her there at A&E. We thanked her manager for taking her to the hospital. The upshot was that Katie was allowed home but was to be kept under observation for the next twenty-four to forty-eight hours. Katie suggested her two flatmates could do this for her and they agreed to do so.

Christine was adamant when we got to the car. Katie was to come home. I sensed the usual battle over who's in charge. I gently suggested to Katie that it would reassure her Mum and me if she gave way on this occasion and thankfully she did.

Thirty hours later she's at home, resting as the doctor ordered. "Have a duvet day" he said. She's fine but tired and has a very sore head.

I cancelled three meetings, and shifted my work priorities to what could be done at home while sitting in the same room as Katie, just to keep an eye on her. Christine did the same.

Mindfulness is being aware at any given moment how you feel, and assessing what is the right thing to do in response to the moment. Sometimes all your plans just pale into insignificance compared to the importance of a new situation. The task of mindfulness is to have that clarity at any moment, not just in emergencies. That's what to aim for.

Blaming and judging

Ultimately mindfulness is about trying to re-arrange our minds so that we do more positive, constructive and enjoyable things in life, and a lot less negative, harmful, unpleasant things. I include thinking in the "things" we do as it's the cause of our actions.

The weekend brought with it the twin competitions of Strictly Come Dancing and The X Factor. It's hard not to be judgemental even just hearing the names of the pro-grammes. "I like...", "I can't stand...", "They were great...", "They were rotten...", "I like her dress...", "He annoys me every time he opens his mouth...".

Now of course as a viewer these two programmes and dozens of other less success-ful but similar ones are entertainment (though some of you might already be mentally start-ing to make a case for critiquing or judging one or both programmes for a whole host of social ills or psychological damage).

But Strictly and the X Factor just reflect in a less spectacular way what we do several times a day. We judge, we criticise, we like or dislike and in doing so we unintentionally re-inforce our likes and dislikes, our opinions, our views, our judgement of others to the ex-tent that they harden and become solid, unbudging thoughts lodged amongst the array of mental states in our heads.

Mindfulness tries to help us to soften

these solid lumps of thought; to loosen them up, maybe even to dislodge them from our mental storage space. This can be greatly to our advantage in daily life, and to all those we engage with, whether at home, work or on the street.

It's very liberating to feel old encrusted habits slowly break up. Somehow we feel lighter, less "stuck" and as a result our world feels less heavy, more flexible, brighter and more optimistic.

This is because, as we start to break up more and more old habits like judging and blaming, the space that develops in our mind perceives things afresh. Often this means we start to see little everyday things with an eye of appreciation and even joy.

The most important category of habits of blame and judgement to dissolve are those that we make about ourselves. Every negative or narrow view you have of yourself is like pulling the walls of a room you're in ever-closer, making the space you live in increasing small, whereas every time you mindfully let go of a negative self-view you push those walls a little further apart. Keep doing this, every day, and eventually you push the walls down and your living space becomes as vast as the universe itself.

Worry, worry, worry

It plagues us, or rather, some of us. Some people seem to have a natural instinct to worry. As ever it could be in the genes, or created by unfortunate circumstances in life, or most likely a combination of the two.

On face value there's a lot to worry about. In our personal lives, we have parents, partners, children, pets, friends to "worry about". Or we worry about the absence of one or more of these in our lives.

Then there's the things we worry about. Money, or the lack of it, debt and the extent of it, future income if we fall ill, or when we're old. Health - ours, our family's. Health scares, nutrition advice, new viruses, Googling common ailments only to discover every common ailment could be a symptom of cancer.

Work, not having work, having too much of it, not liking it, wanting a better job, worrying about deadlines, worrying about pressure from the management, pressure from ourselves.

Travel - worrying about getting somewhere on time, worrying about letting the petrol gauge go too far down, worrying about remembering everyone's passports, tickets, what might have been not done at home when we left it, to what end?

We're frazzled and worn out, more often slowly and sneakily by lots of little worries than the big real crisis worries. This then plays with our mood, our view of life, our frame of mind, the quality of our relationships, our sleep, and so on and on.

It's clear we have evolved to worry in order to prepare ourselves for difficult times. But we're now geniuses at worrying and in fact we live safer and more secure lives than at any time in history.

Be mindful, watch your mind, literally. When it pops up with a worry, try to notice it rather than be smothered by it. Try to just "see" it for a moment or two, then mentally let it pass or glide away. Slowly turn your attention to your breath as we do in our sessions. If it comes back don't get annoyed. Just repeat the practice. Observe, note it as worry, let it go, focus on the breath. Then get on with whatever is best for you in your life at that moment.

Try to be mindful like this as often as you can each day. Just find yourself seeing moments clearly. The results will come but you need to practise.

Managing the Past

A friend's father died last week. Unless you're the first to go it happens to all of us. And our grief is very deeply connected to memories, emotions associated with moments in the past. If the moments were good we are sad that the person is no longer there to share the memory or to be with at all. If the memory is unhappy we can be filled with guilt, regret or remorse, maybe for not saying the right thing to make up or for mishandling a situation and now it's too late.

Similarly we can have long-term pain or blockages because of past events, especially more severe or abusive ones. On a less dramatic level we carry minor grudges, prejudices, dislikes as well as rosy-tinted views of the past. It's really hard to have an objective or accurate view of the past. Memory is not a recorded film of the past but more a remake in our heads.

The important thing is how does our relationship with the past feel in the present, that is at any given moment? Does the past rule us in any way, and if so, is it healthy or not? Through being mindful, through seeing what our view of past events is actually doing to us and our feelings and behaviours, we can learn whether it is helpful or not in our lives.

So first we need to see. Then we need to decide what to do. Mindfulness practitioners quickly realise that there's no point in hoping negative emotions, feelings or beliefs will just disappear, though sometimes they do! What truly matters is how we deal with them. And in 99% of cases the best method is to do what we do in the formal practice of focussing on the breath, namely just notice them, see them clearly enough to give them a name or label, for example, hatred of my cousin because he... Let the feeling fade then just place your attention back to your work—or your breath.

If we catch the moments when we re-live or review the past, and deal with them in a mindful way often enough, we start to weaken the old habitual thoughts and feel-ings. So though they keep popping up un-asked for they are easier to hold at arm's length, and easier to let dissolve into nothing-ness.

We have been shaped very profoundly by our past, our family, friends, neighbour-hood, culture, but the present need not be dominated by this. The present holds so much that is special, fresh, and freely available so it's sad if we don't make the most of it be-cause of being pulled back into an unhelpful past. Treasure those good happy memories of the past but remember it is in the present we live and those tiny moments are the only time we are truly alive. Miss them and they're past too. Participate fully in them, gain all you can from them, give all you can to them, and you will be truly alive.

The Clutha Vaults tragedy

Last Friday night the world changed for some people. Some died in the most unexpected and unforeseeable way. Others narrowly missed the same fate, and still others are left grieving and shattered. Most people living in or around Glasgow felt a personal emotional response to the tragedy and the suffering of the victims and their families.

Mindfulness asks us to take a step back and look clearly without views or judgement on the tragic events in Glasgow.

The first response to this suggestion is a question, 'isn't it a bit callous to look at something so recent and painful in a cool, unemotional way?' Yet mindfulness is a life-long process of doing exactly that, and by doing so, come to a clearer and more insight-ful way of seeing everything in life. This in turn leads to deep inner peace, and much more considerate, kind and effective deci-sion-making in life. So it is worth making the effort even when we feel it is a cold thing to do under tragic circumstances.

The first mindful perspective was one of compassion: it arose in so many of our minds without any effort, a natural, kind, loving response to others' suffering. Surely this is one of our greatest mental traits. It rose in so many of those who were actually in the pub itself, or nearby, to the extent that they risked their lives to try to help those trapped or injured. A truly humbling and awe-inspiring thing to have witnessed.

The second feeling that arose in me requires a cooler analysis, the sense of pride for Glasgow and its people. This was commented on far and wide, and I felt it deeply. However looking back, there is a down side to this response. Are Glaswegians really friendlier and more community-orientated than people say in Lisbon or Frankfurt, to take two cities at random? Is there a bit of ego, a sense of "wha's like us?" about this response?

Most humans have a common feature of caring more about local events than far away ones and we are often biased or negative about other peoples or places. If the tragedy had happened in Edinburgh would those of us who are close to Glasgow have felt quite as shocked or hurt? The day after the tragedy another accident happened in New York. Was our compassion as strong? Meanwhile in the Philippines hundreds of thousands are still suffering from the recent storms.

It is in our nature to consider some people more equal than others, to use George Orwell's famous phrase. Mindfulness reminds us that we have evolved to be like this; asks us if this is how we actually want our minds to respond, and if not, it gives us the insight and space to nurture preferred mental responses to tragic events.

Here & now there are no worries

We are programmed to worry. This mental habit used to save us from wild animals or approaching storms when humanity lived in raw nature. We are also programmed to just be in the moment, to fully absorb and embrace whatever is going on in the here and now with a sense of complete peace, even awe and wonder.

We have these two opposite programmes in our minds. However modern life with its urgency, complexity and distractions has propelled our sense of worry and anxiety to new levels whilst squeezing out time and mental space to see the miracle of being alive in small moments and in little ways.

Mindfulness is a way of bringing ourselves back to the miracle of the moment, the wonder of experiencing real life, right here, right now. Our biggest fear is death, or dying, or the suffering associated with death. The great tragic irony is that worry about death kills the moment. Life is only each moment, and every time we worry about the future we have squashed, eradicated, wiped out our chance to have lived in that moment.

Life is so very precious, and life is only in each of these moments, so each moment is infinitely precious. Worry actually steals your life from you.

Here are three mindful ways of dealing with worry. Try each and see what works best for you. They are to be done as soon as you notice you are worried:

1. When you feel the worry coming on don't suppress it. Note your awareness of it, acknowledge it, even say hello to it. Hi Worry. This way you haven't suppressed it. Then gently but clearly move your attention to your breath and focus for three normal breaths or more. Repeat if the worry returns. Never get annoyed if it recurs, totally accept its presence in your life but don't indulge it.

2. Acknowledge it and speak to it as before. Then turn your attention to what you see and hear, or can touch or smell or taste, right where you are, in that exact moment. Just notice. Stop and sense the fullness of life at that moment. Repeat if worry returns. Never get annoyed at the worry.

3. Acknowledge and say hello to worry as above. Then just observe it directly. Feel its toxicity, its gnawing nature but try not to get swallowed by it. Repeat a couple of times. This way you become very familiar with the worry, and learn to accept and be able to sit with it, thereby loosening its control over you.

Over time you may find that your worry, while still recurring, loses its power and strength. But this is a life-long practice so don't get complacent or lapse.

An anxiety and how I handled it

I've been feeling a great deal of anxiety over the past few days up until this morning. The cause was the crisis in Ukraine and the Russian movement of troops into Crimea.

I have deep family links with Ukraine and these worked against me in terms of the anxiety. My Polish grandfather was captured and held as a prisoner-of-war in eastern Ukraine between 1915 and 1916 during World War 1. In 1922 my father was born in what is now Western Ukraine, though it was then part of Poland. He lived there until the age of 17. Finally in 1939 my grandfather was saved by a Ukrainian from arrest and execution by the invading Soviet forces.

So Ukraine is a personal matter for me as an automatic, instinctive, mental habit. Moreover, I see many parallels between the current crisis in Ukraine and the start of some major conflicts in European and world history... hence the anxiety.

How did I handle it? Slowly and belatedly. It struck me a few times that my mood was being altered by my anxiety about the news, so it eventually occurred to me that a good starting point was to stop watching the news on television. This meant that the anxiety wouldn't be further fed by that source.

Next I started to apply direct mindfulness techniques whenever I caught myself dwelling on the crisis. I'd notice my anxiety or worries, acknowledge them, observe their familiar distinctive qualities; then I'd slowly and directly move my attention to the breath, consciously noting its every quality, and every change.

That brought me back to the here and now. It also brought me back to a conscious realisation that I'm alive, and that each moment of my life actually matters, and from that came awareness that my worry and anxiety are destroyers of these precious present moments.

From there I turned my attention outwards again, to the view from my window. One of our cats, Toto, was on the window ledge outside. The sun was shining on the grass and bushes, and the sky was a combination of white cloud and pale blue. Spring is slowly coming. Flowers are starting to bloom. A light wind blew the branches of the trees, but just gently. You had to pay attention to notice them.

My anxiety vanished completely and it is still gone. Life felt good, I was capable of experiencing fully my own present moment of existence, and I felt strong and able to give something back to others in life.

Finally I wished all happiness and peace to the people in Crimea, Ukraine and Russia.

The mind's response
The Cardinal O'Brien Story

The big news story in Scotland was the allegations against the head of the Catholic Church in Scotland and the UK, Cardinal Keith O'Brien, his subsequent resignation then admission. Few people in Scotland can have remained unaware of the story.

Scotland has had a long and troubled relationship between its two main Christian traditions. Most of us born and raised in Scotland within even a nominally Christian household will have been influenced in some way by this centuries-long religious antagonism. Some of us will no longer share the faith of our parents, some may no longer attend services even if we still adhere to the church more generally, and some will undoubtedly feel differently about the religious divide than their parents.

It can be useful as a practice of mindfulness to try, even after the event, to look into our minds and try to observe what our habitual response was to the different parts of the news as it broke in successive days. Looking mindfully, objectively, non-judgementally at our own response can give us insights into which, if any, of our upbringing, cultural, and school influences still exist in our mental make-up. Asking ourselves certain questions can be helpful.

Did I feel defensive about the Catholic religion or its church when I heard the news?

Did I worry about or expect an anti-Catholic backlash as a result? Did I feel a certain "I knew it" about the case? Did I feel a certain pleasure in hearing bad news relating to the Catholic Church? Was I pleased when he resigned? Did I feel this story reflected something seriously sick about the Catholic Church as a whole, given the previous similar stories? Did I feel "they're all the same" at any time about this case? Did I feel "you can't trust any public figures" as a result of this case?

So often we just respond in a habitual way to news, so habitual that if our family recorded our every response they could predict with great accuracy not just our views about the case but probably even certain words or phrases we'd use.

None of this is to suggest you stop having views about things that happen in the world; only that mindfulness asks us to see how we respond to such stories. Ask yourself, "Is this an objective, fresh response based on reflection or am I just churning out a programmed response that was built into my mind over decades?"

It is also worth asking ourselves about any news item we watch or read, whether learning of this news in any way adds to our quality of life.

Notes to self (write here)
e.g.

1) When I find myself worrying about things in the past that I cannot change or things in the future that may not happen, I must...

PART 3

ACHIEVING WELLBEING

Stress and Tiredness

Stress and tiredness are two different things but each can encourage or induce the other. We usually don't notice we're getting stressed or tired until we're in the depth of it which is unfortunately a bit later than is good for us.

I'm tired as I write this and am aware of the sluggishness that tiredness induces, together with a sense that my patience and tolerance levels are at a low ebb. None of these common human facets are conducive to good.... well to anything good. They dampen your ability to think clearly, to treat others with kindness and civility, and to see the joys of life around us.

The reason I'm tired is that I came down from Inverness on the train this morning, and I find long train journeys tiring. So even without any element of stress the tiredness alone brings on these unhelpful characteristics.

Add stress and we become a long way from the ideal state of mind. So what's best to do when we find ourselves significantly stressed or tired? I just did the following, literally a minute ago. I put my body quickly into classic mindfulness sitting pose—feet on floor, small of back against the back of the chair, shoulders and back straight, eyes closed and took in a slow deep breath and exhaled it just as slowly if not more so. All the time I focused on the breath. I did the same again and the tiredness has diminished substantially. It's easy and it feels lovely even as you do it. Time taken, say forty seconds for the two deep breaths, add twenty seconds to get my body in the right position and the total is about a minute.

After that I did another instant stress and tiredness relief practice. I went outside and mindfully walked slowly around my car. This took thirty seconds. I was aware of my breathing, my steps on the ground, heel then toe, the hardness of the driveway, but also the freshness of the cool air on my face and arms. I noticed a few lovely red and orange leaves that had fallen from the vine above the front door. All pure unvarnished observation and awareness, no intention, no expectation or effort was involved. Result — feeling much more energetic.

It is these little exercises punctuated through your day that can keep larger chunks of stress from building up, and maybe just prevent the onset of more chronic moods like anxiety, depression, or just plain negativity of view. Treat yourself well: give yourself these regular mindful releases.

The pros and cons of routines

We all have our own routines, such as whether we have a coffee or tea in the morning, and if we do, whether that's as soon as we get up or after breakfast. Like everything in life routines can be nurturing, neutral or harmful. A mindful approach to routines asks us how our routines affect not only ourselves but those around us. With the practices of mindfulness we gain the skills and sharpness of mind to more clearly assess the pros and cons of our various routines in life.

As with all mindfulness practices the first and most important thing is to "see". Our routines form one of our most invisible types of habit in life. They are so set we probably don't even see them as routines. We rarely or never stop to reflect on them, so start to keep a little journal of what you do at what time and become aware of the content of your routine day.

Alongside awareness or seeing afresh, mindfulness asks us to be non-judgemental. This doesn't mean we have never to hold an opinion. Rather it means that, at the time we're observing, we mustn't get caught up in views or thoughts about the little routine we're seeing or noting down. We must just observe and note it. Assessing or judging can come later.

Only you can be the final judge of whether anything you do as a routine is positive, neutral or negative in some way. However we know from everyday news and repeated reports that matters such as what we eat, what we drink, how sedentary or active we are, all affect our health. There is also a huge amount of research on what nurtures good sleep and what harms the quality of our sleep.

It is important not to react instinctively to what we discover are our routines. Give it time to settle in your mind once you've started to compile a journal or diary of what the rhythm and flow of your day entails. Don't make sudden changes or resolutions. Just grow in awareness. Let the consequences of your routines sink in.

To give you some wider context of your routines, I have some national figures which I took from an excellent piece in yesterday's Metro called "What is going on in Britain today?"

- 50 million Kit Kat fingers will be eaten

- On average we will walk 4000 steps (about 1.5miles or 20-25 minutes)

- 1 in 4 women will check Facebook at least 10 times

- We will each spend 3hours and 45minutes watching television

- We will drink 70million cups of coffee

- 3.8 million of us will go to McDonalds

- We will each spend 2 hours on our smart phones

The purpose of mindfulness is to help you see reality, your reality, and the reality around you and from that to learn the skills of assessing moment by moment what thoughts, choices, actions, including words you say or write, will nurture your own life and those around you. This includes enjoying yourself and living life to the full. It is therefore very important to be so aware of your daily routines that you can see how they impact on your life and the lives of those closest to you.

One final view from my own personal perspective. I have found over the years that many things I knew were not really healthy but that I "enjoyed" were in fact just routines and acquired tastes ingrained over time. I found, though it took a long time and is still being worked on, that I could replace harmful daily routines and habits with positive ones and in time come to enjoy these as much if not more so than the ones I gave up. The mind can quickly get accustomed to new routines.

Holding a baby

On Sunday I was at my brother's house. One of his daughters gave birth to a baby boy, Alfie, just over two weeks ago. I've always liked babies, so loved it when I was asked if I wanted to hold him.

Alfie has beautiful fine small features and as I held him he slipped in and out of sleep, never uttering a sound, but occasionally looking up at me or around him, and no doubt hearing the noise of people talking in the room.

I loved my short time with him before another relative wanted to take him off my hands. Afterwards I thought of how a baby's mind develops into the adult person we all become. The arguments in science as to how much of our core personality is in our genes, or whether, as most scientists now agree, our genes are able to be switched on or stay dormant dependent on what the baby and young child experiences.

Alfie's early experiences of his senses, what he sees, touches, hears, etc., all soak into his mind, and the love and care provided by his family, plus his unique genetic make-up add up together to give him the pillars of his future personality.

From that starting point we are further shaped and honed by our experiences, and by our response to each experience, so that we slowly become who we are right now through this life-long process. That includes all our finest qualities and all our worst habits or instinctive responses.

Recent research has shown that we can still change our personality, neutralise or even get rid of stubborn old habits, nurture new qualities, and develop positive ones we already have. This is called neuroplasticity. Scans have shown that mindfulness exercises can even thicken physical parts of the brain, just as muscles develop with physical exercises. So we don't have to stay stuck!

The great Japanese teacher of Zen, Shun-ryu Suzuki, taught his students to aspire to maintain an empty mind, a beginner's mind, saying, "an expert's mind sees few options; a beginner's mind sees all."

Alfie, at two weeks old, has a beginner's mind but already it is starting to shape a fixed view of the world. Mindfulness is the practice of shedding the long-held prejudices and automatic mental reactions built up in our minds since birth, replacing them with a clear, calm ready mind, a mind able to look afresh at whatever life throws at us, moment by moment.

In this way we can return to the freshness of Alfie's baby mind, but with the finest mental qualities that life has given us. That is a state of mindfulness.

Do less, live more

We live in a world of almost limitless choice. When I was a boy there were two TV channels, both of which had a children's hour at lunchtime then restarted at around 4pm. TV formally switched off around 10pm then moved to 11pm, finally midnight on a weekend.

Now we have Freeview, where you have the choice of dozens of channels, and if you can afford cable or Sky there's over 100 channels, and most are on for 24 hours each day. Add sports channels, film channels, DVDs, You Tube, and you have endless video entertainments, news and information.

Similarly if you have the money you can go on city breaks or holidays from Florida to India and beyond. Walk into a shopping mall and there's a vast array of clothing shops, from upmarket brands to rock bottom own brands and everything in between. The supermarket shelves are filled with ever more products. New exotic fruits and vegetables are introduced and become commonplace.

It's the same with activities. We can go onto our computers, tablets, ipods, iphones, any type of games machine and we can go to the cinema, bingo, ten pin bowling, night club, pub, theatre, quiz night, and so on.

There's endless choice. On the surface it seems like a dream world. We live a more wondrous life than the pharaohs, than the Scottish and English kings and queens in history, better than Abraham Lincoln or Genghis Khan ever experienced.

And yet...we're not satisfied. We spend all the money that comes in and we fill our every waking moment with work, duties, activities and fun... but still it doesn't fulfil.

The paradox is that humanity blossoms with mental space, with periods of quietude, rest, silence. It's the absence of activity and distraction that lifts us out of our automatic pilot, this habitual unsatisfied state and into a sense of peace and contentment that can border on the serene or sublime.

Have a good look at what you actually do during your day; maybe keep a journal note of it all. Then look back mindfully at it and ask of each activity you've noted "what does this give to my life?" If the answer's nothing or not much you might want to reflect on whether to continue doing that activity or doing as much of it.

With mindfulness the more you give up or get rid of, the more you have.

When mindlessness is a good thing

One of the most interesting things about mindfulness is that it helps you see everything afresh. This means that in the long run you can look into and examine as many facets of your own life, and others, and nature, as time and your growing open curiosity allows.

Without being cajoled into it, or puritanically forcing themselves, people who practise mindfulness often start to see in a new way how they treat their own body and mind. This can often lead to changes in eating habits, relationship to alcohol, attitude towards beauty and self-image, maintenance and nurturing of their bodies, and their relationship to the natural world.

Changes in these directions can come relatively easily with mindfulness if we are patient, that is, if we are mindful enough to recognise our impatience! There's a right timing aspect of this. Push too early to make changes and you can give up frustrated; but wait and wait and wait again, then sometimes something remarkable happens. You just change, and it isn't hard.

Mindfulness itself can help us recognise the right timing to make changes. In classic eastern philosophies this is described as "effortless effort" and once a change of lifestyle or habit is made in this slow, subtle patient way it usually sticks. That's when a form of mindlessness can be a good thing. Automatic pilot is not a bad thing in and of itself. It gets us to and from places in a car without ever once thinking about braking or changing gear. It remembers where the mugs and coffee or tea are when it's break-time.

It's when our automatic pilot clicks in with anger, impatience, prejudiced views, a harsh judgmental negative attitude and matching tone of voice, instant change into stress or anxiety or worry mode, and so many other unconscious mental habits we have that automatic pilot slowly kills the joy in our lives.

Slowly but surely, practising mindfulness in your daily life, you can make acceptance, patience, non-judgmental response, constructive communication even when pressed, non-stress, non-anxiety, and non-worry your new automatic pilots.

Most of our life experience is mental rather than physical, emotional rather than intellectual. Mental habits therefore dominate our whole life view, so if we want to change how we feel about life, work, family, ourselves, we need new habits that "see" the world differently but still realistically. This is ultimately what mindfulness gives us the opportunity to do. So keep doing it...

Addictions and harmful habits

On Friday evening my wife and I were invited to see a band play at a pub in Bridgeton. It was a charity event for a respite centre for homeless people, primarily those who have been drug addicts and, in most cases, had spent time in prison.

When the band took a break, three of the users of the charity's services spoke in turn about their life experiences. Each talk was brief but moving, all uplifting. They had found help through the charity and, eventually, paid work.

By coincidence coming home this morning from my mindfulness class I passed the local health centre and saw two men come out. They had the same aged, harmed faces as the people who spoke at the pub, the same slumped body posture. I had seen them before at the chemist and knew they were addicts who regularly received methadone or some other substitute drug.

Such harm, such pain for the addicts and those around them, particularly for their closest family members. Theirs is a most public, and most judged sign of a harmful habit, a compulsion.

Of course, all of us have an innate tendency to develop habits and to crave "things". It's just that some have worse effects than others. It would prove very useful to our lives and those around us if we examined our own inner and outer world more closely. What habits do we have? Do we crave anything? A holiday? A lottery win? Retirement? A job? A better job? Chocolate? Wine? Ask yourself What does my craving feel like? We might find ourselves automatically asking, when does a craving become a habit, and when does it become an addiction? I think it doesn't matter. We can get caught up in a wilderness of opinions on such things.

What matters is the effect. Do any of our habits impede us on our life journey? Are any of our cravings inherently harmful to us if we indulged them? Do any urges or cravings or habits make us needy, dissatisfied with life, negative, judgemental, unpleasant company to be around?

The practice of mindfulness slowly allows us to look progressively deeper at the many layers of wants, moods, emotions, prejudices, desires, longings and deep-rooted unhelpful habits we possess.

That's why the practice is so important; sitting quietly and focussing on the breath; or just walking and seeing where the mind instinctively goes. We get to see our positive and negative mental traits. Then we can start to neutralise the destructive ones, and build, appreciate and nurture good ones. Try it today, become aware and start the process of mental transformation.

Deprogramming, reprogramming

From the point of conception right to these passing moments we are programmed and are constantly being reprogrammed. Some of us were born quick to anger, others laid-back. Our life, our culture, where we were brought up and by whom has made us feel Scottish or Czech or whatever nationality. It has made us think of the world in Christian, Muslim, atheistic, scientific, or other ways. Every single aspect of our personality, our traits, our beliefs, our likes and dislikes, our prejudices and loves, have been programmed into us either through our genes before we were born, or by every single experience we have had up till now... including the effect of reading these words.

We're all different because of this process, yet we share two things of great importance in common. Firstly none of us consciously chose our mind or our personality. We have just had to accept what life has given us. Secondly, and more importantly, we can do something about this. We can gain, slowly but surely, a great degree of control over who we are and what we think, say and do. This is the great opportunity that mindfulness gives us.

In neuroscientific terms it's called neuroplasticity, the ability of the mind to be tweaked, adapted, adjusted consciously and deliberately, even when we are old. Research on mindfulness practitioners has shown that regular practice can even change the physical structure of parts of the brain, just as exercise develops bigger muscles. Other research has shown that certain parts of our gene structure can be switched on or off if we practise regular mindfulness.

Therefore, our experience of clarity and calmness when practising is not just subjective; change can actually be happening to physical matter and at gene level.

Mindfulness deals with both parts—the deprogramming and reprogramming of our minds, our traits. It deprogrammes through learning not to be attached to or taken over by certain destructive or distracting emotions or thoughts. We don't suppress them, we merely observe them and in doing so neutralise and disempower them.

Mindfulness also reprogrammes. Being quiet and observing the present reprogrammes the mind to notice more, and not to accept everything the mind produces. But more than this we can use mindfulness to deliberately cultivate calmness, clarity of thinking, compassionate feelings, a self-nurturing attitude, and other healthy traits.

So although we had no choice over the genes we received at conception or the myriad of beliefs and habits we've gained through life, we can now choose to remake ourselves differently.

Acceptance of trauma

One of the key aspects of mindfulness is not to judge in the present moment or "now". But what are we to make of this when something happens which we instinctively feel is... well choose your own favourite word:

awful
terrible
evil
disgusting
disgraceful
shocking...

This could refer to something someone has done to you, to a member of your family or a close friend, or it could be your response to an item on the news, or simply a feeling that arises when someone tells you a story.

Don't we have a right to be angry, feel hatred or dislike for the person who could do such a deed? Even more strongly, shouldn't any decent person feel the same way, meaning that if you don't get angry or riled then there's something wrong, uncaring, immoral about you?

Mindfulness does not ask that we stop making distinctions between right and wrong behaviour, our own—and others. What it does ask us to do are the following steps:

1. Become aware of what you are feeling in response to the news or incident.

2. Observe your state of mind, what you're feeling, calmly and gently, not allowing yourself to get swept up in the mood or emotion.

3. The process of becoming consciously aware then observing what your mind has created usually softens the mood or feeling to some degree. From that less heated perspective you can then ask yourself how the mood or feeling helps you or others in any practical way.

4. Only then are you in a clear and peaceful enough frame of mind to know whether anger, judgement or c o n d e m - nation is helpful or not.

In my experience, and yours may be different —emotion that moves you towards animosity in any way towards a living thing or person is rarely helpful, especially as it helps form new mental habits similar to the one you just expressed or felt.

On the other hand expressing in a calm, sympathetic way to the person who has been harmed or upset by another person that you feel what the person did was terrible, awful etc. may very well be appropriate because you are now using the judgemental words to make the other person understand that you feel for them. You don't have to experience the negative emotions to use the words in a sympathetic way.

As ever it is all about each unique moment and you have to be the one who makes the decision.

Dealing with difficulties

Last week started well. I was on the Sleeper train down to London for a major meeting with the UK Business Secretary Vince Cable to discuss how best to help family-owned businesses, but when I got to London my wife called. She had had chest pains, and tingling in her arms and hands.

I got on the next train north and thankfully she was given the all-clear and allowed home twelve hours after she went to A&E.

On Wednesday it was our cat's turn, he had to be checked by the vet to assess his level of kidney failure. Turns out it's low level so can be managed.

On Friday my daughter came home from a city break in Gdansk. She broke up with her boyfriend of three years the last night of their holiday together. That pain is not so easy to medicate.

Also on Friday my aunt's nursing home phoned to say she had fallen in the kitchen and split her head open. Nasty, but much more serious when you're 95 years old. Thankfully she too is well.

Life's like that, totally unpredictable. Things can be rosy for years then there's a flurry of crises.

There's a lovely old Indian story about a farmer who steps on a thorn when walking barefoot in his fields. He goes to complain to the elder in the village, "Why can't we cover all the paths with leather to stop our feet from getting cut and wounded?"

The elder said, "There isn't enough leather on the earth to cover all mankind's paths but if you put the leather over your own feet you will be protected."

Mindfulness is putting the leather round your feet. It protects you from the worst of what is inevitable in life, like the week my family had. I practised mindfulness for almost all the five and a half hour journey up from London, calming down my fears and anxieties about my wife's heart scare.

But mindfulness has something extra that leather doesn't have. Not only does it protect you against the worst of worries and emotions, it nurtures loving, kind qualities so that you can reach out when needed to help put some leather round the feet of those near you.

We are only on this beautiful Earth for a short time. We need to learn as quickly as possible how to protect ourselves from our own worst responses to life's ups and downs and this world would be transformed if we could all learn how to give just a little bit of protection and kindness to others.

Make hay while the sun shines

It's a beautiful sunny Monday morning as I write this. Being Scotland I don't know whether it'll still be shining in an hour's time when I head off to my main meeting of the day.

That phrase, make hay while the sun shines came to mind. It's a call to action, a call to appreciate and make the most of things while we can and in the big sense of life and death, it's a very important point. At the end of this strange, complex thing called life is our death, and after that, well that's another big discussion altogether. What we do know is that this life we have ends and there are no more moments in this world to experience.

Thus—all the more reason to work on honing and cultivating the highest qualities of yourself through mindfulness. These moments we have, whether one or a million, can be completely missed if we live in automatic pilot mode, mindlessly reacting to everything that happens with old ingrained habits. We can sharpen our awareness, our attentiveness, and learn to master the remarkable but often self- harming minds we have.

If we do that, we can not just seize the day (carpe diem) but can find incredible richness in each moment, in tiny little things like the way a shadow falls across a road and onto a grass verge, or when a family member laughs at a joke made by a comedian on TV.

The scientific truth is that the sun is always shining. It is just sometimes hidden by clouds, and at other times it's shining in Asia or Australia while we're in bed sleeping. But it's always there, shining, bringing warmth and light to our world.

In the same way, despite the presence of heavy clouds or deepest darkness, our minds always have the capacity for peace, calmness, happiness, love and kindness. These qualities are embedded in our genes but sometimes the negative habits and traits which are equally part of us hide these more refined qualities.

Mindfulness is a way of gently dispelling the clouds, the dark moods, and allowing the sunlight of our positive mental qualities to shine inside us. We need to exercise these healthy mental states every day, and we need to keep gently letting go of our destructive qualities, not aggressively, not angrily, but with a sense of quiet even kindly persistence.

The truth is, a sunny day is not beautiful or otherwise, it just is. Similarly a murky cold rainy day isn't horrible, it just is. As Shakespeare wrote in Hamlet, "there is nothing either good or bad but thinking makes it so." Gautama Siddhartha, the teacher known as the Buddha, said, "with our thoughts we make the world." So work to make the sun shine in your mind.

PART 4

PRACTICES

Four mindful actions for each day

Mindfulness isn't just about sitting still for 5 to 20 minutes observing the breath and seeing what's going on in your mind. The greater opportunity, and ultimately the whole point of mindfulness, is to fully experience the moment as it occurs, and to respond constructively and warmly to whatever that moment brings into your life. Your ability to do this, to hone your mind so that it is alert enough to do this more frequently, can come from trying regular simple tiny practices each day. Here are a few, but you can do this with literally everything you do, say or think.

1. Waking up and becoming mindful.
When we wake up we are not mindful; we're scarcely awake, often groggy. It can be very helpful to just ask yourself when you are sufficiently awake, what is my mood like right now? Just watch your mind and see what it is actually like. If it's unpleasant, grumpy, negative, see if you can just bring a tiny bit of sunshine or a wee smile into the mind. Nothing major, just the slightest move towards a happier frame of mind.

2. Your first bite of food in the day. Whether it's toast, cereal, whatever, just try to be fully aware of the whole experience of that first bite. The texture, is it crunchy, smooth, soft? The taste, is it subtle, mixed, or in your face, sweet, savoury? Enjoy experiencing that first bite. The rest you can just chomp!

3. Same with your first drink. Whether that's water from the tap, tea, coffee, orange juice, just experience it as if you were examining it like a scientist trying to discover its full properties. Is the cup or glass warm or cold in your hand? What does the drink feel like at your lips? Is it pleasant there or does it have no qualities at your lips? When it goes into your mouth does the flavour burst out at once or emerge more slowly? Can you savour the flavour or does it come and go in an instant? Is it strong, subtle, a mix of the two? Does the flavour change or intensify as it goes toward your throat? Is there an aftertaste? If so, is it a great taste, nothing special, unpleasant? Again, no need to do this with every sip, just the first. Experience it all. It can be done in ten seconds flat, but it's a full ten seconds.

4. Tidying the kitchen after you have eaten. Once you have eaten look at the

kitchen and the plates and other things that need tidied up. Check how your mind responds to this situation. Are you irritated? Down? Neutral? Whatever frame of mind you are in, try to just watch it then let it slowly go on its way. Then if you have time just methodically, not in a rush, put away one thing after another, and try not to do more than one thing at a time. If you put your dishes in a dishwasher, try doing just one dish or piece of cutlery, smoothly, carefully, enjoying the simple process of putting something in the right place easily. Then the next and so on until they are all put away. Likewise if you wash the dishes in the sink, try to enjoy the simple wiping job, then the straightforward rinsing and placing onto the side of the sink.

That's it. That's real mindfulness, real practice. In these very simple everyday ways you are training your mind to remain calm and appreciative, alert but relaxed. Keep doing normal routine tasks in this mindful way and you'll be surprised at how quickly and practically you start to become mindful not only of the little things in life in each moment, but of the big things too. You'll find that you are on top of your mental state when more challenging things crop up. After all, being aware of the experience of a cup of tea is actually the same thing as being aware of when you are grieving, angry, petty. It's all there for you to be aware of, observe it, and decide whether to engage it or let it gently pass.

Handling that unhelpful inner voice

Sometimes the least helpful voice is our own. The one that says, when it's cold outside, you don't really need to go for that run, that bike ride, or even to visit your aunt in the nursing home.

It's the voice that tells you it's ok to have another glass of wine or pint of beer when you've already told yourself you'll stick at one because you have to get up early the next day. And it's the voice that tells you that a caramel wafer is so much better than an apple even though you're on a Weight-Watcher's diet that definitely said "apple" as your snack for the day.

There's no point in speculating why the mind has evolved to be so unhelpful in these ways. That just leads to a debate which can never arrive at any conclusions, so it's a waste of time.

One of the key principles of mindfulness is to accept what is. We all have a mind that often tries to scupper our plans to do what we know is best for us. Just clearly accept that this is the case.

However, accepting reality isn't the same as doing nothing about it. It's just the starting point. The second principle is never to get annoyed at reality. That's kind of pointless too. Getting annoyed, angry, ranting, or unhappy about anything doesn't help the situation, it makes you feel bad, and worst of all, trains your mind to be more ready and able to feel those negative feelings in a similar future situation. Not the sort of mental training you'd choose.

The next step is where true mindfulness comes in. This is to be clearly aware of where your mind is heading. Even as the thoughts arise - "eat that lovely Tunnocks wafer" or "it's too wet to go out" - notice its arising. This is what mindfulness actually is, the pure sharp awareness of what your mind has produced as it is doing it, real-time awareness.

Then on analysing objectively what your mind has come up with this time, gently but firmly assess whether this is a helpful, neutral or unhelpful thought. If it's neutral or helpful go with it.

If you perceive it to be unhelpful, remember not to get annoyed with yourself or your mind, just give it a name or label (eg. biscuits—or putting things off again) then allow the thought or emotion to just gently fade away. It does most of the time.

Now you have a clear mind. Make a clear, positive decision e.g., no biscuit but an apple instead. With practice this becomes easier, and you start to feel you're winning the subtle battle with your inner voice. That makes all the difference.

How to do the dishes...mindfully

Let's face it. Most of us don't like doing the housework which is a pity because unless we own Downton Abbey we just have to get on and do it.

I've watched my mind while doing the dishes, sweeping the floor, ironing, mopping, dusting, cleaning the toilets and bathroom. Does my mind like this regular routine has-to-be-done work? No.

My mind tends to do one of three things while I do the housework. Mostly it thinks ahead, of the work I've got to do after finishing the housework. This might just be a simple totting up of what's on the 'to do' list for the rest of the day. Or it might go deeper and start to plan some of the steps of a task.

Next most common is daydreaming. Remember that lovely beach in Turkey? The mind wanders to it, then something triggers a mental leap to my days working in the Western Australian Desert, which makes my mind think of Australian beer and the colour of the beer cans they had. I can even taste it. The last main area my mind wanders to is moaning. "I hate dusting" my mind tells me. "What a mess. Can they not keep their stuff off the floor?" or "They should have put these cups and plates in the dishwasher before leaving home this morning."

I'm good at moaning and so I should

be. I've been practising it for decades. Same with daydreaming and constant planning. Rationally, these are very strange things to practise yet many of us are geniuses at moaning, daydreaming, planning, planning, planning.

What if we stopped indulging these mental muscles? What if, instead, we practised focussing on the task in hand when we did the housework? What if we practised being grateful that we've got a home, a brush, a mop, an iron? What if we practised being appreciative of the skills we have to do these tasks, or the limbs and hands and fingers and muscles which we use to do them? Imagine just doing these simple little mindfulness exercises every time you do housework. Just pure attention to the detail of the work. Add some gratitude and appreciation. Imagine practising this every week for the next couple of decades. What would happen?

Your mind would make you a genius at focussing, maintaining attention, feeling grateful for being alive, appreciating the little everyday things in life. At the same time your moaning, daydreaming, obsessive planning mindsets would quieten down, maybe disappear. How different would you feel?

So let's stop moaning about it and treat housework as a genuinely amazing way to develop happiness and wellbeing.

Here. Where you are right now

Are you in any way affected by where you are? Its warmth or lack of it? Its fresh air or lack of it? Its lighting, colour, atmosphere, or lack of these? Your past experiences of here? Can you change any of these? Probably not. Do you allow these features of here to affect your mind in a negative way?

It is an unusually warm muggy day here. Probably the same where you are. If people living in Scotland were to be happy and energised only on warm days we'd be dour for over three hundred days a year.

Mindfulness asks us to be aware of how we are feeling, what we are thinking at each moment. Often our frame of mind is instinctively affected by our surroundings, by "here". So learn to be aware of here. Then with mindfulness practice, with pure calm observation and insight, we can slightly shift our attention to see what is good about here. What is to be appreciated, enjoyed, admired, what we should be grateful for about here.

Although we are so used to it that our instinctive mind tends to see nothing positive about where we are, most of us are under cover, with heating, technology to help us do our work, transport, private or public, to get out or home. Most of humanity doesn't have those things. They are not "here" in their lives. Even the most famous and wealthy people of history had nothing compared to what we take for granted here. It is accurate to say that you have more essentials and luxuries, of better quality and efficiency than Roman emperors, Popes, pharaohs, Marie Antoinette and Napoleon. Do you appreciate this? Can you perceive afresh with mindfulness to attain this insight and appreciation?

Mindfulness can help us see what we truly have here. Stop every so often and really look, mindfully, at where you are at any given time of day. Here is almost always special. You just need to see it.

A New Year to nurture yourself

We have the tradition at New Year of making resolutions. Then we usually have the follow-up tradition of breaking those resolutions and adding a third tradition, feeling bad or negative about ourselves because we couldn't even keep a simple resolution. Thus a good thing becomes a negative thing and spawns a poor view of ourselves.

There must be a better way of improving ourselves than this. The reality of course is that there is no such thing as a New Year. It's just something created by us as we developed society. A year is simply the 365 days it takes the Earth to go round the sun (plus a little bit more which we add as a Leap Year every four years to keep the arithmetic on track).

Every day is the start of a New Year compared to 365 days previously and as mindfulness is all about living right now in the moment, we can say that each moment is a New Year compared to that corresponding moment a year ago.

Why write this? Why dwell on what seems to be irrelevant? Looking at our lives and time in this way allows us to achieve two very important things.

Just let go of a resolution that we've broken the moment after we break it. Don't think twice about it. Let it go. Let go of any disappointment as if you are letting go of a ball in your hand. Just drop it. It doesn't matter anymore. Then in the next moment make a new resolution. Keep letting go of your annoyance when you break any resolution. Then keep making new ones for as long as you live.

This might seem pointless but it's not. As you make a positive resolution it seeps into your brain's store of thoughts and ideas and it strengthens your resolutions slowly but surely. You are in essence building a mental muscle, one which supports your resolution.

Though it seems like you're getting nowhere, you are in fact making steady progress, and you're not berating yourself either, so you start to feel better about yourself, and more at ease with your life.

The periods between breaking resolutions may start to stretch out, and maybe, just maybe, you'll finally crack one or two of them... without effort, without a sense of draining force of will, just by letting go when you break them and then by sheer easy repetition of making the new resolution.

Try it, keep renewing resolutions and of course make practising mindfulness one of your key resolutions too!

Practice, Practice, Practice

Mindfulness is such an interesting and huge subject that we can be caught up in learning about it instead of practising it. This is like reading all about nutrition and healthy foods while continuing to stuff ourselves with crisps, biscuits and cakes.

It's difficult to establish good habits. Bad ones seem so much easier to achieve. So to help here's a very quick, simple but effective mindfulness practice you can do every day and it only takes a minute or two. In fact you could do this two, three, ten times a day it's so easy.

Just sit somewhere. Don't bother with the more formal mindfulness techniques of sitting upright or scanning the body to make it more relaxed. It's much more important to just do the practice.

Close your eyes. (That takes away all visual distractions). Focus on the breath. With your first in-breath say slowly to yourself the words "my mind is clear" then with the out-breath say in the same slow quiet way "my mind is calm". Next breath do the same but say the words a bit more slowly. Third breath, reduce the words to two single ones, clear for the in-breath; calm for the out-breath. Slow and long, more like cleeee-aaarrrrr and caaaaaallmmmm. Repeat that for the fourth breath if you have time. Fifth breath repeat the words and visualise with the in-breath that your mind is completely empty, bright and shining clear as a bell. For the out-breath picture your mind completely still, as if time has stopped; there's nothing but your peaceful mind.

Sixth breath repeat this. Seventh breath just focus on the breath. No words, no images. Eighth breath, say to yourself "I wish happiness for me, for everyone, and for everything that lives," then slowly allow your eyes to open.

That's less than two minutes and it does wonders. You don't need to do all these breaths. Any two or three is enough to work. You could record yourself saying the instructions I've just written and play it so you can be guided without having to check. Or ask a friend to say the words for you and you can do it for them in turn.

Sitting still in the evening

We often find ourselves tired in the evening, whether we work during the day or not. And it has become a very common habit to sit if not slump on the sofa in front of the TV, usually with a glass of wine or other drink.

There are four interesting points about this way of "dealing" with any tiredness or stress from the day.

1) It's not really dealing with the tiredness or stress at all even though it feels like it.
2) Sitting in a slightly slouched way does not rest the body but just shifts muscle tightness from one place to another. As we know from mindfulness sitting practice a tired, uncomfortable body makes it hard for the mind to settle and relax.
3) Television is anything but relaxing or revitalising. Instead it is a constantly changing series of incidents and conversations at a time when the mind would most benefit from quietness or some level of gentle consistency.
4l) Your glass of alcohol affects your mind's ability to pay quiet attention and relax. Alcohol depresses the ability of the mind to sit quietly and still.

So all told this default method of letting go of the day is highly ineffective and may in fact compound over time the very stress and fatigue we're looking to get rid of.

As an alternative try to find, or ask your family if they can give you, a quiet space for just five minutes.

Sit upright as in practice, feet hip width apart, hands on your lap, eyes gently closed. Just observe your breath lightly but clearly, the freshness in the nostrils with the in-breath, and the warmer pressure of the out-breath. If the mind wanders just note that it has, then go gently back to the breath. Never get annoyed at distractions. Just accept them. After five minutes or so just allow your body and eyes to slowly come out of the practice and get back to normal.

Try that for a few days this week and see how it compares to your usual habits in the evening.

Five thoughts to reflect on

I reflect on the following sentences every morning when I wake up. I do it while I'm still in bed so it's easy. You might like to use them too as a starting point but over time explore exactly what frames of mind you'd like to have to begin your day then write and use your own.
Here are mine.

1. I am grateful to be alive and able to eperience this new day.
2. I feel at peace with myself, with my place in life, and with the world even with all its faults.
3. I wish happiness and safety for everything that lives.
4. I will nurture my body and mind today.
5. I will try to bring joy and full attention to every moment and to everyone I meet today.

Those people who know me best know that I don't attain these states of mind, but I do move more in their direction because I started my day not just reading or saying these statements but spending a minute or two reflecting on each and using mindfulness to try to cultivate the states of mind that these five sentences represent.

I hope you find this useful and gain benefit from it.

What am I thinking, feeling now?

Just observe your mind. Try to see what frame of mind you're actually in. Could be you're tired, focussed, down or cheerful. Don't try to judge it or change it... yet. Just notice it and look at it for a few moments.

Try to perceive it in some detail if you can. Notice if the state of mind was one you expected to have, was something you had chosen, or if instead it at some point just popped up and took over what you wanted to be thinking or feeling. Just notice all this without analysing, assessing, judging. Just allow these observations and insights to settle in your mind—these exercises are all helping build your mindfulness capabilities.

Once you have seen clearly where your mind was or still is, now you can ask yourself the important questions:

a) what would I like my mind to be like right now?
b) where would I like my mind to be placing its attention right now?

See if you can find inside yourself the state of mind you want to have, maybe by visualising it, or thinking of some past event or possession that brings such a feeling to your mind.

Or maybe it's just as simple as going for a break if you are tired, or breathing consciously for a minute, or simply refocussing on your work or task. Turn your eyes and mouth into a smile too, that often changes our states of mind by itself.

I did this exercise this morning when I awoke and got up early, around 6.15am. I was swithering between doing some work or going out on my bike but on looking at how my body and mind felt, decided it was better to go a short walk. So I did a mindful walk for about fifteen minutes. No one was up, the world was quiet as I walked over the wasteland area at the back and around my home. It was very peaceful, a light drizzle, but I had a coat on so that didn't bother me, It was actually quite pleasant. As a bonus I saw a long-tailed tit on a tree, and a young rabbit.

Most of all I did what I'd learned that my body and mind would benefit most from after observing them gently and quietly for a few minutes. It made for a lovely start to the day.

How are you feeling right now?

Just pause for a moment, close your eyes once you've read these first few lines. (I'll tell you when to stop reading.) You may not be in a position to close your eyes so it's also ok to do it with eyes open. Think to yourself "How do I feel right now? What is my mood? My frame of mind? My attitude?" Give yourself enough time to see it clearly. At first you might just think "I'm feeling nothing." Or "I'm ok." But be patient, look gently but clearly. You might find there's a heavy concentration, or a slight frown, or a real pure focus. Perhaps a little down, or maybe quite cheery. Try to see it mindfully, clearly, without judging it – but do give it a label or name.

Stop reading now and do the exercise.

Now consider the fact that you didn't ask yourself to be in that frame of mind, that mood, those feelings. Your mind just created your mental state through its own remarkable process, one in which we rarely play a part. Mindfulness reminds us that this is the default way the mind operates—outwith our conscious involvement. Mindfulness enables us to see our state of mind. Then we can ask ourselves, "What state of mind would I like to be in?" and equally importantly "What state of mind would those around me like my state of mind to be?"

From this we can then think of certain things that might help move the mind towards the preferred state. For example in my house just now we have some lovely tulips in our living room. Just thinking of them, or visualising them, makes me happier, more upbeat, cheerful. Doing this removes me from my previous state of mind and takes me quite a distance towards the more actively happy frame of mind I'd prefer to have.

Try it for yourself. Once you know what frame of mind you have and which you'd prefer, you can start to think about what object, item or thing might help shift your mindset. For some it might be a child or baby (maybe your own), maybe a pet, or a landscape you love, a happy memory. Whatever it is, just try to find that frame of mind, and once you have it try to feel it fully, try to let it become your new default position. This is a very simple practice. It often works, but like all things in mindfulness, sometimes it doesn't. Sometimes it works for just a minute or two, other times it changes your whole frame of mind for the rest of the day. So do give it a try.

Making everyday moments mindful

Sitting in silence and observing your breath and the way your mind actually operates is the core of what is called mindfulness practice. However if you want to shift your brain's habits from automatic pilot and negative responses to situations then the real practice is to try to be mindful at any moment.

Here are some examples:

1. When you wake up try to become aware of what mood you are in. Don't try to change it, just notice it without judging. Then once you have done that you can maybe try to raise a wee smile or think a positive thought to shift your frame of mind a little. It's amazing what this small practice can do to change your day.

2. When you shower or clean your teeth try just being fully aware of doing it and how your body feels about it. Don't judge it, just be aware of what is happening and how you respond to what is happening, both physically and mentally.

3. When driving, focus on driving, not on the radio, ipod, CD, daydreams, planning work. See how you might instinctively reach to put the radio on, even a minute after deciding to be mindful of driving instead. Old habits die hard and your mind wants to be in charge of

you! At red lights focus on a single in and out breath. Just be aware. Then notice the clouds, any trees or shrubs, people, shops, all without judging—this is pure awareness. On the bus or train you can do this more freely. You can even engage in sitting quietly and observing the breath through the whole journey.

4. When you get to your destination be mindful of your walking to the building you work in, the atmosphere of the office or workplace, the temperature, the mood of your colleagues, your feet on the pavement or floor as you walk, your breath as you walk. Just notice.

Thus, before even reaching your work-place you could have completed four, five, six or more mindfulness training practices. The more we practise the more we establish new constructive mental traits and the more we heighten our mindfulness so that we see our ingrained unhealthy states of mind just as they begin to arise.

Now try it... and keep on trying it for the rest of your life

With grateful thanks for the support of

The Scottish Mental Health Arts & Film Festival

www.flemingpublications.org.uk